99
Pot Stills

Bill Owens
American Distilling Institute

Bill Owens & Andrew Faulkner, Photography
Gail Sands, Pica Graphics, Design and layout

© 2011
White Mule Press
distilling.com

LIST OF PHOTOGRAPHS

INTRODUCTION

The POT STILL

The foundation of the craft distilling industry is the pot still. In recent years the design of the pot still has gone through "moderation" with the addition of the rectifying column. This addition allows distillers to produce products that they could not before by just using a simple pot still. For instance, with 14 plates in a rectifying column, you can make vodka. There are now over 350 craft distilleries in the USA, and almost all use a pot still.

The photographs in this book started on a "journey" in 2006 to "see" America. And on this journey I visited some craft distilleries and photographed some pot stills.

Then came another trip across the USA, visiting and photographing craft distilleries. I later took a third trip across the US photographing distilleries for the book *Whiskey and Other Spirits*. After this book was completed I realized I still had 100 unpublished photographs of craft distillers and their distilling equipment—the pot still. This book is the result of having driven over 33,000 miles and visiting over 100 craft distilleries.

Bill Owens
President of American Distilling Institute

45th Parallel Spirits

AEppleTreow (Apple True) Winery & Distillery

Alltech's Lexington Brewing & Distilling Co.

Amalgamated Distilling, Jake Jones

Anchor Distilling

Bainbridge Island Distillery, Keith Barnes

Bardenay Distillery

Balcones Distilling, Chip Tate

Balcones Distilling, the grant

Mosby Spirits, Bill Mosby

Batch 206 Distillery, Jeff Steichen

Black Heron Spirits

Brandy Peak Distillery, Dave Nolan and his dad

Breuckelen Distilling

Bull Run Distilling

Catoctin Creek Distilling

Cedar Ridge Distillery

New Orleans Distilleries

Clear Creek Distillery, Stephen McCarthy

Maine Distilleries, Chris Dowd

Colorado Gold Distillery, Tom Cooper

MASH STILL

S.N.1   500 GAL.

Copper Fox Disillery, Rick Wasmund

Crown Valley Brewing & Distilling

Desert Diamond Distilling

Distillery 209

Domaine Charbay Distillery, Marco Karakasevic

San Luis Spirits

Koenig Distillery and Winery

Shelter Point Distillery

Cahill Winery, Don Payne

(Licensed) Experimental still, David Mahaffey

Domaine Charbay Distillery, Marco Karakasevic

Empire Winery & Distillery

Ernest Scarano Distillery, (l-r) Darrin Critchet & Ernest Scarano

Essential Spirits

The Filson Historical Society (museum)

Flag Hill Farm, Sebastian Lousada

Forks of Cheat Distillery, Jerry Deal

Forward Brands

Garrison Brothers—(l-r) Fred Koch, Dan Garrison and Fred Koch.

George Washington Distillery

Grand Traverse Distillery, Kent Rabish (left) & George Wertman (right).

Great Lakes Distillery, Guy Rehorst

Greenway Distillers

Harvest Spirits

Hidden Marsh Distillery

High Plains

House Spirits

Huber's Starlight Distillery, Ted Huber

Indian Creek Distillery

Jaxon Keyes Winery & Distillery

Dutch's Distillery

Leopold Bros., Todd Leopold

James Whelan, Head distiller at McMenamins Edgefield Distillery

Middle West Spirits

Modern Spirits

Nashoba Valley Spirits, Richard Pelletier

New Deal Distillery, Tom Burkleaux

North Shore Distillery, Sonja Kassebaum

Old World Spirits, Davorin Kuchan

Ranger Creek Brewing & Distilling

Parch Group, Paul McCann

Peach Street Distillers, Davy Lindig

Pennsylvania Pure

Philadelphia Distilling

Prichard's Distillery

Privateer INTL., Andrew Cabot

Rock Town Distillery, Philip Brandon

Roughstock Distillery

Ryan & Wood Distilleries, Bob and Cathy Ryan

Shellburne Orchards, Nick Cowles

Solas Distillery

Solomon Tournour Distillery

Sound Spirits

Spirits of Maine

Square One Brewery & Distillery, Steve Neukomm

St. George Spirits

Stillwater Spirits, Don Payne

Stillwater Spirits, Jordan Via

Stoutridge Vineyards

Stranahan's Colorado Whiskey

Sweetgrass Farms

Thirteenth Colony Distilleries

Tom's Foolery

Triple Eight Distillery

Tuthilltown Spirits

Uncle John's Cider Mill, Mike Beck

Valley Spirits, Lee Palleschi

Richland Rum, Jay McCain and Erik Vonk

Belmont Farms, Chuck Miller

Westford Hills Distillers

Woodinville Whiskey

Victoria Spirits, Peter Hunt

CPSIA information can be obtained
at www.ICGtesting.com
Printed in the USA
262896LV00007B